FEATHERING DEEP

FEATHERING DEEP

DAVID M. PARSONS

Texas Review Press
Huntsville, Texas

FIRST EDITION, 2011
Requests for permission to reproduce material from this work should be
sent to:

Permissions
Texas Review Press
English Department
Sam Houston State University
Huntsville, TX 77341-2146

Acknowledgements:

I wish to express my gratitude to the editors of the following journals
and anthologies in which poems from this volume have or will appear,
occasionally in different versions: *Agave, a Celebration of Tequila An-
thology, Borderlands: Texas Poetry Review, Descant, Louisiana Literatu-
re, Numinous Magazine*: Spiritual Poetry, *SWIRL: Literary Arts Journal, The
Criterion, Concho River Review, The Langdon Review of the Arts, The
Texas Review*

As with my previous books, I owe a special debt of gratitude to Paul
Ruffin and the staff of Texas Review Press, whose support is inspiring and
gratifying. I have also been extremely fortunate to have had the gifted
editorial advice and friendship of Jean Wood.

Many colleagues, mentors and friends; old and new, have given me
support, ideas and memories that have been instrumental in the crea-
tion of the poems for Feathering Deep, including in no particular order,
Laura & Keith Doehrman, Mark and Dr. Brandy Parsons Miller, Robert
Cunningham, Kerri Nowell, Allison Paige Parsons, Cliff Hudder, Edward
Hirsch, Stanley Plumly, Janna Patrick, Patty Winn, Susan Portis, Phil de
Masco, Kathryn and Van Wood family, Paul Mariani, Jeanette Kierbow,
Jack Wilkes, Shirley Schwaller, Father Hubert Kealy, Rusty Wier, Fred Han-
na, Dr. Terry Parsons Smith, Donnie and Jerry Parsons, W.D. Parsons, Jeff
and Juaneva Jamar, Bill Wenzel, Terry Barnard, Robert Leffingwell, Steve
& Jane Thompson, Craig Campobella, Bert Hofer, Richard Howard,
Robert Pinsky, Howard Moss, Cynthia MacDonald, Lisa Ziedner, Wendy
Barker, Dianne Logan, Dr. Richard Griffin, Paula Teague, Dr. George
Boyle, Deseree Probasco, De De Fox, Dr. Kenne Turner, and always,
my mother Reba Lanet Kierbow Parsons who turned me on to reading
books one lonely summer in the rolling woods of Austin, Texas.

Library of Congress Cataloging-in-Publication Data

Parsons, David M., 1943-
   Feathering deep / David M. Parsons. -- 1st ed.
      p. cm.
   ISBN 978-1-933896-79-3 (pbk. : alk. paper) -- ISBN 978-1-933896-80-9
(cloth : alk. paper)
   I. Title.
   PS3566.A769F43 2011
   811'.54--dc22

                                    2011023293

For Nancy

CONTENTS

IV

I

FEATHERING DEEP

After Edward Hirsch's
"The Angel and the Demon"

I believe it to be
unlike any other
conveyance

the manner in which
it carries us in
upon its own silence

the way an idea drifts
into the grey divide
where we find ourselves

in that sacred state—easing
quietly into the dark *duende*
to unconscious understanding

a lone canoe at midnight—blades
paddling deep—smoothly
and deftly feathering

that largest of bodies

FIRE

After Jo, La Belle Irlandaise (Johanna Hifferman)
by Gustave Courbet

At first glance, Johanna Hifferman appears
to be brushing her stunning long red hair,
hair filling the frame as it forms her looming
intense face, where dazzling blue eyes blaze
into a hand held silver mirror, as the other
hand toils at fiery ringlets, petite fingers pulling
gently from atop the creamy painting of brow
above the magnetic passion of those eyes,
eyes drawing the looks of the crowded queue
all gawking like the awed bystanders watching
some grand building aflame, their attention
keeps returning to the two small windows, where
humanity might emerge, showing its true
face, some emotion, like fear, despair, desire,
lust, emotions they might all recognize within
themselves or their outed longings, all standing
like worshippers before some magnificent
cardinaled saint, like Joan herself, burning,
flaming...inside and out...all present—blessed
with fire.

EVENING AFTER EATING RAINBOWS
(CAUGHT ON MYSTIC LAKE)

A mostly found poem—for the Van & Kathryn Wood family

Bohumil Hrabal wrote that every beloved object
    is the center
of a garden paradise
    and everything that lives
must have its mortal enemy—
Lao-tze said that to be born
    is to exit, to die is to enter—
Rimbaud wrote that the battle of spirit
    is as terrible as any armed conflict
and Kierkegaard said you cannot separate
    the slimy from the golden fish
(without killing the fish)—
    in a polluted river running
through stretches of factories
    a beautiful fish may sometimes
be found sparkling like an eye—

Once a man collected books on aviation
    because he thought Icarus
was Jesus' forerunner—
    are we all like olives: only
when we are crushed
    do we yield what is truly
the best in us—
Inquisitors burn books in vain—if a book
    has anything to say, it burns
with a quiet laugh, because
    any book worth its salt points
up and out of itself—

When we were young lovers
    so transfixed
with the complexities, especially
    of the sensual body
we had to say everything
    with our hands
In the starry firmament of night
    the senses lie dormant,
an immortal spirit speaks
    in a nameless tongue
of things that may be grasped
    but not described

After an evening considering all these found
    thoughts in your small body of fire,

I could easily coil inside myself
    like a cat in winter
but it is midnight and I am back
    on the outskirts of Absarokee, named
for the Crow, looking directly above,
    into the ebony wings of an unambiguous
Montana sky, my head arched up—
    and out—spinning—spinning—
in *Too Loud a Solitude*—

FALLING

After a laboring climb up the fifty finely honed
        granite
steps entering the Blanton Museum's beginnings, I
        find you

falling to the robed rock, as if you might have just
        kicked
a goal or been pushed roughly down by playful
        schoolmates.

Perhaps, you are taking a short breather before
        rising again
to the playing field to exact a young man's prankish
        revenge,

your four limbs, though, somehow erecting the
        vacant air—
left short, accentuating the missing hands...
        missing feet—

your face with that innocent, youthfully blank
        expression,
like the game face of players of all the serious
        contests of man.

The nameplate above identifies the body, yet,
        inconclusively
as *Dionysus or Heracles* and states, you are a copy,
        expendable

in a way...merely a casting from the ruins of
        Parthenon's Circle

of Pheidias, yet, in finding you here in Austin on
    this unhistoric
sweltering June morning of 2008, I am wishing for
    a place to fall, sit
and recover, not from the climb—from the single
    chilling inescapable

thought—you are neither the god of wine missing a
    wistful hand
holding forth a marbled cup, nor the son of Zeus—
    today

I am reminded of agonizing images on the news
    from Walter Reed Hospital,
our own young Marines and soldiers falling back
    home to us—not unlike

warriors of every century through the many stair
    stepping years of history—
we always think of time as progress, moving up
    toward the lofty air of gods,

yet, here, this moment, I find myself witness again
    to a player such as you—
cast as a casualty of civilization's latest stumble—
    after all these centuries,

we are still falling—

WOLF ATTACK

Western Art in a Cloudcroft Café

The eye first finds
a cowboy turning

'round—the pace, loose
couplets of thought wolves,

not the deep sounding
of the whirling snowy

storm in the ominous dark
we all share

framed in the vortex
of our inner weather, our

own unique ambushes,
the confined chaos, a circling

trail of claw prints
we cage within—all

the things in our head
left unsaid—

PORTENTS OF INSCAPE

Someone once said you must kill a poem to dissect it,

yet, I find blades of life here: the word, *portent,*
may be an indication that something unpleasant
is about to happen, perhaps, a personal prophecy,

omen or a wonderful and marvelous thing—destiny?

and inscape: the distinctive and essential
inner quality of something, especially
a natural object or scene in nature

like the manner in which a poem resides

curled within the intricate intertwining
of the yin and yang of the many writers
so fecund of all the enigmatic possibilities

for something new, fruitful,
an entity
lit from within.

KITES

Death is such an awesome
experience that it takes
your breath totally away.

I wish for this poem
to be the antithesis, under
stated, even modest

like simply breathing,
yet, indispensable
like the brisk breezes

holding colorful sails
against clichéd blue skies
or the breath that sends

aloft the many shaped lively kites
like student aspirations, dreams
tied to the determined fists of hearts

with the almost imperceptible strings
of hope, perhaps, one climbing a bit higher
with the small wind of this poem.

I wish this poem to breathe—

HEARD ONLY AT POETRY READINGS

Because of the church like atmosphere of most readings
any sound made is first perceived as rude intrusion, not
this sound, which could be someone clearing one's throat
but for the few of the audience that chime in guttural
  unisons

Uumm

It could be the reaction of someone asked to choose
one's favorite Emily Dickinson or Walt Whitman
poem to read before a crowd of accomplished poets
and scholars Pub-full of the spirits of Walt, of Emily
Or perhaps only the assessment made by a thoughtful
person in making most any difficult decision like
which dessert to choose from a really fancy tray
of treats: Chocolate Mousse, Cheese Cake, Crème Brûlée,
Chocolateb . . . yes, yes, it is like chocolate or pancakes
or perhaps, the compliments of a new friend or suitor
in that the number of times it is actually heard may
somehow, begin to negate its value to the palate

Uumm

Or the same utterance made by lovers in the beginning
ecstasies of their pyrotechnic first touch and mindful
awareness, the oblique sensations of sexual contact.
Yes, it is that first discovery of a rare entity—a taste of
  a body.

Uumm

II

TEXIAN

Colonel Juan Almonte, Santa Anna's aide, was the first
To call his attention to the heralding of two golden stars
Floating in the familiar field of green, white and red
Over that unlikely mission fort Alamo, small stars
That foreshadowed the larger single searing symbol
Emblazoning our ultimate flag of Texas independence
We fly so proudly today. And each of the banners
That flew over the those many battles, all spoke
With the same unwavering intonation, No!
No, we will not become minions! Imagine with me
The cacophony of these many varied accents,
Of Kentucky, Tennessee, Louisiana, Alabama,
And Tejano, lilting together in the casting throng,
A composition of the most unlikely of battlefield
Symphonies, a timpani for independence.

Walt Whitman wrote in his Leaves,
They were the glory
Of the race of rangers, matchless
With a horse, a rifle, a song, a supper,
Or a courtship, large, turbulent, brave,
Handsome, generous, proud, affectionate,
Bearded, sunburnt, dressed in the free
Costume of hunters, not a single one
Over thirty years of age.

These were the men and boys
Of whom Walt called the jetblack
Sunrise at the last battle Goliad,
The same ebony tinted sun that fell on
The hardened rough hewn clay arch
Of the hallowed battlefield Alamo, where
Within the brawny breastworks of both
That simple chapel complex

And the ragtag men staged within
Was mirrored these same
Uniquely Texian traits.

Texian, Texian, Texian, the word
That soon returned a jetblack siesta
To the soldiers of Santa Anna
In the far flung fields of beach brush,
Mesquite, live oak, and pines
Of the San Jacinto battleground,
Texian, a word immortalized
Now the world over
By the actions of these gallant few.

Yet, these were seemingly ordinary men
With common everyday problems, desires, prejudices,
Fraught with human frailties, not ideal or perfected.
It is said that even General Sam Houston
Years before these momentous days,
Standing deeply depressed perched
Top deck on the river boat *Red Rover*,
Was saved from a suicidal fall by the sudden
Flash of auburn plumage as an eagle, a Cherokee
Omen foretelling a greatness to come, swooped
Auguring down toward him—

Today we stand with one of Houston's resurrected warriors
So perfectly formed by *Campobella's sword*, ennobled
Amongst these thirteen flags, not an hour's drive north
Of where his grand triumphant destiny brought us ours,
Where the wafting fragrances of salty gulf coast breezes
And the pungent smoke of gun powder sweated the air
That breathed life into the fledging hopeful breast
Of a stately body to come, making legend these hallowed
Winged emblems now fully realized, as our omens,
Their bright feathers forever woven with the blood
Of these many iron willed, uniquely, soulful
Menagerie of men: these Texians.

BLINDS

After John Graves' Goodbye the River

I have languished
in the chill
of a deer stand
at dawn in wait—
watching for those
jeweled eyes

to wander through brush
land trees—sleek auburn
presences lithely moving
through the dawning
air, rich with the hot
stink of life, as

I huddled damp
in the steam of my
own heat, the bluing
cold of my riffling
dark on dark—in
the swirling shadows
of the last fading

of evening's many
deaths, slayings that
went without a report
I could discern
in my blind of artificial
trees, and yet, I
am, also, a witness

and citizen of the ancient
tribe, that coalition

that exists in the universal
chain of fear
and food—the aiming
eyes behind our many
individual stands—
all narrowing our sights,
those many faceted irises,
eyes we see through—
not with.

THE PEOPLE

"Though they became known as Comanche's,
they called themselves Nermernuh (The People)."
                              The Handbook of Texas

Their ancestors thought
the wild flying geese
to be red-eyed white
hounds harrying
damned souls across
the evening skies—

I imagine them standing
in a trance like state—
seemingly dumbstruck
by the sight of the furious
flights of those many small
hearts beating ruby hope
against plumed breast—

not unlike small flags
flying in formation
behind some unnamed
leader who from afar
looks no different
than the last lagging
harrier waving wildly—

and here, tonight
those spirits fret about
me in midnight's bed
reading—vivid stories
of bloody raids against
the emerging white menace—
clouds of covered wagons—

each crimson episode
another of history's
many tragic tales
of failed preemptions—
the image of that wild gaggle,
so fluent of air and time, returning
again and again and again

the way the scarlet rimmed
eyes of the past always
infiltrate our present—

MIDNIGHT MONTANA: LITTLE BIG HORN

Standing
in the middle
of this ancient hallowed
battleground,
my head arched awkwardly
humanly skyward, hands
and heart outstretched
and flat against the icy
north wind, a wind
like the timeless ocean,
knowing no Alpha or Omega
looking upward
 like all men, all women
making their stands
in the centering surrounds
of their own personally
flagged arenas—unseen
arrows pinning them
to imperceptible crosses,
my mind is shot through
with the searing thoughts
of the many wars, warriors coming
before me to this very moment
and there begins
the spinning within
the grand gyre,
my corpse-like ogle
meets the icy ravishing eons:
starry eyes in ebony winged skies,
winds like the myriad of murderous
ravens flapping, flapping
an echo—this must have been
the true sound of the coming
of the Valkyries—

INTEGRATION 1964

When James Brown's band
or most any Motown Group,
hits one of those ecstatically high
shrilling passionate sax notes, sweaty
Phil, tie loose, is swimming *The Gator*
on the gritty dance floor at Charlie's
Playhouse in after hours' deep East Austin,
when it was the "bad part of town"
and we were like giddy young tourists
and I can taste wee-hour fried chicken
from nearby Ernie's Chicken Shack
and recall how we were always too high
to worry about the rumor of sleepy cooks
spitting into our honky customers' gravy
& mash potatoes, we were flying our lives
through the sixties and we didn't have a clue
that we were like the Ugly Americans.

HILLS

For the men of the 1st Marine Division (Korea)

Driving to Silverton
from Durango, we
survived the mountains—

harrowing hairpin turns
and steep shoulderless
massif grades that plunged

us white-knuckled to
another hilly hairpin turn
and after an anxious hour

a tiny town, a camp
of dollhouses still far
below us, dotting

the valley like some
grand idyllic village
and in the late evening

I finished reading
THE DARKEST SUMMER,
a book mostly about Marines

of the Korean War
and how they survived
hill after bloody hill,

because the war seemed all
about the capturing of this hill
or that hill, and the intense cold

at the Chosin Reservoir
that caused their weapons
to freeze, so that when

thousands of Chinese came
in darkness surrounding them, they
could only toss hand grenades

down the hill or up the hill,
it was always about this hill
or that hill

and the maps in the map rooms,
of the Generals on both sides,
these hills all had numbers

and the numbers were piles
of other numbers and they
were like the piles of bodies

that were collected on both sides,
because, they could not bury
them, because the ground was frozen

so they had to make piles of bodies
until they could blow a big grave
into the side of a hill to entomb them.

Warfare has always been intolerable
for the infantry, not like the wars I played
at over forty years ago, a Marine Reserve,

never actually capturing a fortified mount
or defending a crucial hill, just enough
war gaming in the barren California

mountains and the scrub brush of Austin's
foothills to give me a small notion
of what another Marine "Grunt" might

have been feeling in actual combat,
and tonight, alone in my camper
in this scenic Colorado mountain

valley retreat, I cannot escape
those 1st Division Marines
of that historic battling flight

from the icy Chosin Reservoir,
their stories are frozen in my head
and as they were totally surrounded,

they are imbedded in graying hills,
springing up in dark ambushes
of my thoughts; and I remember

my own Drill Instructor preaching, how
fire superiority can overcome any hilly
fortification, explaining how the 1st escaped,

because every Marine is a rifleman
and each time those Jarheads squeezed a trigger
a Chinese soldier went to the cold hard ground,

and I keep thinking that it must have been something
else as well, because they were so outnumbered
and it was so frigid, and there were so many, many

hills, there must have been something burning
deep in the valleys of the very essences
of their individual beings, some other kind

of unique fire superiority.

I WOULD GIVE YOU THE SINGLE STRAWBERRY

Not because it is the end of May: the season—
or that in the 17th Century William Butler said,

It is doubtless God could have made a better berry,
but doubtless God never did; or that the delicate

uniquely heart-shaped berry has been heralded
through the ages as a symbol of purity, passion

and healing; or because of Shakespeare's adornment
of Desdemona's hankie; or that Madame Tallien

of Napoleon's court would crush 22 pounds in a fine
basin and bathe in the glory of the luscious ruby juices;

nor because of its shape and color, it was the symbol
for Venus: Goddess of Love; or that it was widely held

by Romans to alleviate symptoms of melancholy, fainting,
kidney stones, halitosis, attacks of gout, liver and spleen;

not even the legend that if you are lucky enough
to have a double berry and share it with one

of the opposite sex, surely true love will follow;
not even that they are the only fruit carrying their seeds

boldly on the outside like the regality of knights of olde.
I would give you the single strawberry as a kind of
        communion

offered in recognition, remembrance and celebration
        of our brotherly and sisterly spirits;
moreover, as a reminder: strawberries are not

harvested with machines, their small bodies
being so very delicate, human hands must carefully
harvest each berry;
and as we savor it, let us meditate together on the visions

of the multitude of pickers—people like you and me—
bending
under brutal sun in the rote of work, taking each
unique berry

with measured grace, with reverent aplomb—I would
give you
a single strawberry because, despite all that has perished

and been lost the past year, we
have lived to see...to taste another glorious spring!

III

THE MARRIAGE LOST

When everything that could fall

has fallen

there will always be two hearts hanging

obscure, deep in the gristled harboring breasts

of us hawks

floating in the constant wind of timeless memories, poised

in the heavy pewtered sky of our two minds—

there is no true end

to this parting that we have lived with so many years

and now, like two intrepid birds of prey hunting

in different territories,

we have in common our differences and the blood

of our blithely fey times together—still pumping wild

in the deep craw

of the ancient machinery of the feathered crafting

of our individual lives since, and residing subdued—

deep within me

endures the lofty vision from these high altitudes of
    a time— there

now...that small brown speck in your morning green
    eyes,
                                           eyes—

that with one blink of the thought of them, a bright
    portal opens,

a drumming heart—a catch of breath—still singing
    the sweet
                                 turbulent tones

of our times—swimming in the brine of that one eternal
    orbit—

                                 suspended—

EVIDENCE

When I leave the musk
of your most intimate

auburn presences—
flipping myself out

from our common
flannel cotton sheets—

we ritually secure
ourselves between—

instinctive individual
attempts at preservation

of mutual heat, our
melding moments—

then stumbling out
and up to the rude realities

of the bathroom's
utilities—honking
chrome, cold medicinal
green tiles and stoic toilet—

I sometimes notice
a trace of you, a hair

perhaps, curled along
the sink bowl's curve

or a smear of make-up, cherry

giving blush to the chill—
life to the white sterility—a hint
of the evidence of you—signs

of daily shared presences—proof
of the us...the undisputable: we are—

I think of your complaints of the daily
mess—I am fraught to wash it away.

LOSING SIGHT

A stroke should be drama—surely pain—
I thought it just a wink that went wrong,
like morning eyes, a temporary blurring
shadow, a problem with the mechanism
a glitch with the softest part of the hardware.
A small error that surely could be corrected
with wonder drugs, perhaps super eye drops
or a precise laser shot to the correct nerve.

It was a blink
that changed
everything
leaving me
no peripheral
vision.

That I could lose sight forever
with such nefarious subtlety,
makes me wonder in random moments
at all that might have been lost to me,
in that same innocuous fashion,
much of which I didn't even realize
had been missing—
the many hours, days, years,
precious minutes and seconds, so many
of my children's lived moments, while
the dark shadow of personal ambition moved
me through thunderous life, spending
countless time squandered—now embarrassing attempts
to pass the many pointless, worldly eye exams, to find
some charted societal recognition—a vision of success,
sadly living my every days with that one benign
        blind spot.

SIXTIES MUSIC

When the oldies radio station plays,
I Can't Get No Satisfaction... memories

flaming hot fire-up, flashing sensual scenes—
Susan, waking me—on the family-famous brown

couch in my parents' Rollingwood home, where
I had crashed after partying until the wee hours

following another late night Lifeguard cleaning
session at Barton Springs, our boom box at the max

as we wrestled a fire hose, blasting the basic beginnings
of algae from that ancient limestone creek bottom—she,

stretching her bountiful Scandinavian body smooth
against the length of mine, bringing me alive,

slowly, with the smell of her shampoo, nuzzling
damp morning-hair...and later, that one wild

all night driving of her from Austin to Baytown,
dangerously winding around each other, hands

wanting to be everywhere at once—attempting
to keep my old grey fifty-seven Chevy in tune

with the streaming white lines of the highway,
our heads bobbing, lips all musk and Mick Jaggerish

in the gamy steaming young music of our bodies.

STEPDAUGHTER

The term has always felt clumsy in my mouth
not unlike the relationship at its beginnings—

the tangle of families that creates those awkward
first hugs—so full of mixed emotions—histories—

I remember the first time I was struck full face by the
        joyful
blue-green eyes that were plumed in that small face
        surrounded

by the shock of blondish brown hair...a mane that
        seemed
much too substantial for a child's head—redolent of
        thick, lush

texture of the mother's—hair that I remember hurriedly
        brushing
those early school mornings into shiny bouncing
        dog-ears—

stunning locks in complicated snares and rats,
        demanding gentle
concentration, occasionally evoking a snagging yelp
        and pain

reflected in those eyes—distinctive, subtly different
        from her mom's,
yet, with the same unusual mesmerizing qualities.
        Those first blurring years

were the times the awkward nature of the term was
        truly onomatopoetic

of the relationship—countless hard encounters of
     miscommunications
and cobbling of minds and wills, and then euphoric
     discoveries—selfless
moments—genuine feelings of family—the years have
     passed and like roots

grown in buried tangles under a grand old oak trees,
     all the those complicated
nerve endings, so raw from being torn from their
     original bodies, have found

their ways to firm new ground—rich loam—step...
     daugh...ter...the term,
as in introductions, still does not feel correct to my
     dumb tongue—my daugh...ter,

two smooth syllables combed together as two pig tails
     woven carefully around
each other—naturally: *I would like you to meet my
lovely daughter, Laura—*

FRIED GREEN TOMATOES

I cannot recall one conversation I had
with her, just the cool dignified kindnesses
when from Texas I visited her tiny neat
modest Bremen, Georgia home with photos
of Liberace placed as one might display
important family members or iconic leaders

maybe saints; the sumptuous fried green tomatoes
she introduced to me one day after returning home
for lunch from a morning of sewing on the assembly
line at her life-long Sewell Suit Factory job, yet, her
neatly modest and homely presence, after over five
decades of not having seen her, returns at unexpected

times, her jet black hair and awkwardly attractive
tall rangy angular body with those remarkable eyes,
those icy agates set in that smooth pale oval face,
eyes that seemed to look directly through you
as brown eyes, with all their warm charm
seem never to do . . . like the difference between

the kindred eyes of dogs and the inescapable
and ineffable combination of chill and thrill
that is stirred subtly deep within our own animal
depths, when unexpectedly one might glance up,
finding his gaze has become locked in—frozen
by the rapt mystical hunter eyes of a stunning cat—

now an enduring memory of that first titillating tug
of the visceral, formative instincts of the fine keening
of the pure quintessence of discovery: new, green—fruit.

THE EDIT

Reading a poem to an audience, years
after its having been published
or even revisited, I discovered a word

that should have been another, an edit
that was so obvious to me—the apt word
stealthily entering my consciousness—

I stumbled over it, embarrassingly
losing my train of thought, nervously
shifting my weight, pussy footing—

my feet doing a little dance, behind
the speaker's stand, my mind
in a state of reorganizational panic,

as when the face of a former lover, emerges
from memory and lightly touches something
strangely new, something ethereal, causing

a deep stabbing regret, a strange mourning of the reality
that has set that old relationship—eyes, mouth, legs,
          nuances,
into permanent grey fonts of memory: the finality of
          inky script—

wishing with a small aching remorse that one could
          at least,
reconnect—to attempt to rewrite the ending, an editing
          deep
down in the sinews comes—the painful finality of the
          error—

this flawed personal publication, this misprint in the
intimate canon—
I cleared my throat and looked at the audience with a
nervous smile,
the false wry smirk of a minimum wage department store
clerk, forcing

the move on...the next word, the next line, another
poem—Robert Pinsky's
long forgotten comment now comes to mind, "We always
publish too soon."

IV

READING OLD HEART

I have been diving
into your heart
for weeks now
like some lone bear
returning to a kill
not always directly—

meandering through
your *meandering* through
trees that are rivers—branches,
alive with Magpies and Blue Jays,
many, many Jays, and Spirit Birds
taking me to more water, streaming

rivulets that run like blood, life's
milk from the many varied sources,
observations of the natural world, blood
being always present, inescapable
while feeding, head and heart,
rib deep in that divine carcass

of your minds eye, bloody
run off from all our carnivore
hearts is everywhere I look—
I know, I know there are butterflies,
flowers, an abundance of flora,
the heart-felt human conditions,

and I should be feeling Keatsian
and I do, but I can't help thinking, too
of that massive tome: Ted Hughes.

CHURCH GOING SESTINA 2010

I am thinking about Phillip Larkin's uniquely
      masterfully
penned poem, *Church Going*, a chillingly cynical
      musing
about churches and what they may become when
      all faith
has left us all to the hard, hard wiring of the
      coming Tech age.
I am in the third row of St. Joseph quaint old
      Catholic Church
in Fort Stockton, Texas and Father Manimala's
      compelling voice

sounding of India, flows sublimely over the flock,
      rapt in his voice
and witnessing the total acceptance of this
      diminutive Asian's masterful
celebration of the Eucharist in a mostly Latin
      American church
dotted with us few white faces I am struck with my
      own musings
about the viability of the universal global message
      in our exigent age.
Will these small communities, braced with a few
      foreigner's faith

endure the onslaught of the discursive information
      age, where faith
in any thing unseen has become superstition? The
      stark reason of voices
of reason is what remains, leaving wanting the
      grown-up children of our age
to wander back into these old sanctuaries with that

subtle hunger for a Master
to rekindle in their being the mysterious assurances
    of the inward musings
that might help clarify their lives. Behind and above,
    the choir fills the church

with *God Bless America*, as it is the 4th of July and
    the small church
is similar to all Catholic Churches in our country,
    the icons of a faith
in all the usual places: a large crucifix with Christ's
    last pain, musings
hung on a large mural of blue sky, a stand of pines
    giving subtle voice
to community inclusion, alabaster family table,
    Lamb relief: Master
carrying the flag of peace besides the matching
    A+Ω lectern: ageless

symbols in the timeless atmosphere stoked by the
    past seekers for our age.
So Phillip, I think, yes, just as you said it *pleased*
    you to stand in the church
of your poem, the many souls born since you posed
    your querying masterpiece
and the unborn to follow, will keep coming, seeking
    some sort of fruitful faith
to quell the raw hunger that you also perceived in
    us and so eloquently voiced
those many years ago; and as I recall the tone of
    your words again, the musings

are tinged with the slightest bit of a wonder, perhaps,
    a passing curious musing
of what it would be like to have allowed yourself an
    opening even at your age

to the possibility of the impossible, to have entertained
    the intimate inner voice
that has whispered to the wisest of men, bringing
    them dazed to some church,
as you said, to *a serious house on serious earth,*
    where green groundless faith
may be discovered, nurtured, blossoming within,
    filling the dull void, mastering

the mindful muse that must reason, icy analytical
    thinking, finding no true church,
only aged *frowsty barns* for storing the hewn
    imaginings of those few faithful,
yet, that querying murmur remains: *in death, might*
    we be the master?

INSCAPING THE STORM

For Hubert Kealy (1938-2010), after Paul Mariani's
Gerard Manley Hopkins: A Life

He once said to me, if the Christ
splendor had not seduced him,
he would have given himself
to the Lady Literature, his mind
to happily spin in the sweet Irish
gyre of his genes—his heart of mind
is still and forever will be pierced
by Gerard's grandeur, his body joyfully
churning with the oceans of inscapes
filled with blessed blood, propelling,
priming life's profundities through
the ardent aspect of a saintly eye,
and just as now, I remember him

standing tall on the very anniversary
of Hopkins's vows, a stormy Feast Day
of the Assumption, he is at the wheel
of the holy galleon, Sacred Heart Church
and he—is— the eye in pandemonium,
like that bold lioness nun of the doomed
Deutschland, he centers himself
in the Mass, our majestic main mast
cloaked in the sails of his creed,
flying our colors proud, despite
the keening cancerous plague,
the waves of chemo nausea,
the agonizing baneful babble—all
landings within his sight fraught
with the wrecking rocks of ruin, yet
he stands amidst the brunt of it, his frail
alb clad jib raised—strong on high, chevying

chaotic, chthonic born winds, proclaiming
against all darkness, to all above, all below
and to us huddled around on hallowed deck,

This is my body . . . this is my blood . . . .

LAKE LADY DANCING ON THE HILL

Above the south shores of Lake Travis
she moves in the dawn that is breaking
over the railings of the house that clings
to the ancient limestone cliffs—she is the deep
and complex aroma of a dark, rich coffee held
in both hands against gusts of wind that have carried
a chill across the water, a body so deep and blue
that it captures all the light intense morning sun
can send against the hill country valley fortified
with green plumes of Texas plant life barricading
the giant furrow—the sides of the vast aqua catacombs.
Like that steady open vein that flows below, she will
be still moving in the evening that has broken over
that same ornamental ironwork for years, saving
the crow's watch of a porch that juts artfully from
the brow of the hillside she loved, she is this grand house
that will always bring joy to the hearts of memory—
to those lucky travelers that found themselves in her
respiteful inn of light and laughter for a day, or maybe
a weekend—for an, *anytime*—for she is the mother
            of joy,
she is the girl dancing and singing glory on the hill top
high above the water that like her mind, looking so
            calm
on the surface, is always eternally sounding our
            depths,
she is that energy that makes all that surrounds
            resound.

SPRING SUICIDE

In spring the cars of light begin their trips, plotting
    Their way through thin grey solenoids
Of fall, where tall shadows have been eclipsed
    And dappled skins of green reclaim the voids.
Winter leaves town dragging its dark, soiled pale
    And a sixties Chevy rubbers the winding trails
Of the cold shoulders of Mount Bonnell, leaning
    Into the spin high above Bee Creek, the
        wind, no rail—
Through safety glass appears a lost young smile
    Winslow Pratt's red-faced Howdy Doody
        simile
Speeding through the hair-pin turn, flying
    Into my poem as my first deathly dark memory.

KNUCKLE BALL

We were a true blue baseball family.
Not that we didn't care for football or basketball,
we loved all the sports. The ritual begun by
our traveling salesman father, a former pitcher,
we would listen to the Yankees and Dodgers
on the radio—he loved Pee Wee Reese—and then
he would hit us ground balls in the front yard
on those slow hot Austin weekend days, the rare times
he was home from pitching Higgins Slacks on the road.

It was the only activity, I can recall, we did solely
with him—the single thing he would happily do
with us without a strong urging from our mother.
My brother Donnie was the best...glove hand magic
in retrieving the worm burners Dad would hit at us
from across the sidewalk that cut the yard in half
and often would give the ball an extra little hop
to be dealt with, as we would try to go to one knee
blocking positions, as he always coached us to do,
to make sure that if our hands were too slow or
we faltered in our judgments, our bodies would
make the stop—take the blow—thus saving a hit
to the neighbor's driveway or worse, the street
taking the ball down the steep incline of the hill
to the wild surrounding thick cedar country woods.

Our father never showed overt partiality to Donnie,
however, his body language and his hazel eyes gleamed
the pride in my brother's innate skills and though I
      think
our youngest brother Jerry was too young to perceive it,
I remember feeling a twinge in my chest, in the vicinity

of the heart, a painful plunk of envy, like one of
     those bad
hops—my father, he could throw a perfect knuckleball,
a deceptive pitch that comes at you surprisingly
     slow, vibrating
weirdly, creating an allusion of the ball's true path—
     true purpose—
I could hit his knuckleball—his best pitch—better
     than anyone.

TWO DOGS HOWLING AT THE MOON

for Rusty Wier 1944 -2009

I will always remember the last time I saw you,
at your *angel's,* Tricia's crowded Plano townhouse

and how, after our four hours of harmoniously
catching-up on thirty some odd years of lost time,

I read you my poem *The Pride,* about that pack
we ran with—we thought we were lions, we were

more wolves or stray dogs—reliving those old stories
of growing up together wild in the enigmatic sixties

in South Austin, like our Tequila drinking contest
when I came home from the Marines, how I passed

out hearing you strumming to *Rave On,* learning
later, you had quickly followed me to the darkness

falling dead-drunk onto your beat up old guitar,
like some faithful warrior falling on his sword.

As our visiting ebbed, you played for me the second
of your three new songs, saying, *"I'm still writing—*

*can't stop doing that one thing—we're like those two
old dogs in my song, David, we writers just keep barking*

and howling at that ole' moon," your voice still
inimitably valved despite the chemo and the thousands

of songs poured out like manna to the many hungering
audiences of the nightlife you so loved and I remember

at that moment thinking how Li Po is said to have so
adored that great luminous orb that he perished, when

after a night of heavy drinking, he fell into the lake
attempting to embrace the dazzling antediluvian body,
    tumbling

head-long and alone into the deep ink of oblivion,
or perhaps, the masked reflections of an eternal light

and how you, after sailing through countless gigs
and seas of Agave, one complimentary shot at a time,

were now arduously floundering to make the best of
    each
of these last painfully clumsy egregious moments,

like you always have, with that distinctive dancing
twinkle in the weathered squint of those smiling blue

eyes, eyes still fully alive in my memory, still dancing—

I suppose every human passion holds within its core
the germ of something lethal to its being and yet,

somehow, interwoven with the potential of rapture.
Tonight the sheer linen curtains of my bedroom seem

to be tossed by the blurring energy of the moonlight
bouncing glowing stones across the dark water of
    our pool

as the ceiling fan circles in its perpetual waving orbits
and I can hear my daughter's tiny lap dog underneath

my small dinghy of a bed gnawing like memories
on a T-bone scrap from dinner, he is at that phase

where all the meat is flayed away and one can only
hear the sound of bone against bone as he is working

into a rhythm in his ceaseless mastication, creating
his own unique kind of wild, raw and satisfying music.

TRAIL MARKERS

Every first Monday of the month
you would pick us up, 6:30 P.M. sharp

for Boy Scout meetings: Troop 1
at the O. Henry Junior High gym,

my school, the same space I learned
to dance in socks, doing the two step,

and how basketball was a kind of dance
from five foot tall, Coach Herman Wiese.

My traveling salesman Dad never being home,
your zeal was the only thing that kept me

in Scouts, you made it so easy, always
picking me up for meetings, weekend camps

and then helping me in securing a summer job
teaching Canoeing and Rowing at Camp

Tom Wooten. I remember how you would
go out before our camping trips and leave

Indian trail markers for us to find and follow
and how to make wild berry tea and survive

eating plants and grubs. Time and again, I
have found aspects of the ideal man in small

examples you planted in my head; in five decades
I never thought of you not surviving anything.

You were the most honest, self-resourceful man
I had ever known. I can see you now, tanned,

tall and slim with graying temples, impeccable,
Atticus Finch in a Scout uniform with your

ever present, Eagle Badge and knee socks.
After the Scout meetings, we would always
play a pick-up game of round ball, while

you would pack up the scout stuff and re-clean
what we had missed in our half-hearted attempts,

though firm, you never ranted or raised your voice.
On the way home we would frequently stop

At Scotty's Bakery, where I would buy a dozen
hot, out of the vat glazed donuts and wolf down

the entire bag before being dropped off.
After all these years, I can still feel

the huge knot of sugar, grease, and dough
tightening my gut, not unlike the feeling

I had when my old, fellow Scout Bert told me
you were gone and I had missed your funeral,

and yet, even if I had been there, it would have
been too late to tell you what I regret never saying,

simply, Thanks, Mr. Wilkes, I do not know who
I would have become without having known you

and after all these years, I am still discovering myself
in memories of your many edifying ways, trail markers.

NOTES ON FEATHERING DEEP

FALLING

An ekphrastic poem composed for the Blanton Museum Poetry Project at The University of Texas. The art triggering the poem, was a casting from the ruins of Parthenon's Circle of Pheidias *Dionysus or Heracles.*

PORTENTS OF INSCAPE

A phrase found in the Ange Mlinko review in *Poetry* entitled, "How Devin Johnston and Linda Gregg Chase the Romantic."

KITES

Originally title was "Occasion." The poem was composed at the request of the student editors of *SWIRL: Lone Star College Literary & Arts Journal* for their 2008-2009 issue, which they dedicated to me: a high and humbling honor.

HEARD ONLY AT POETRY READINGS

I owe the idea for this poem to Susan Briante after hearing her comment on the sound intimating from her audience while reading one of her poems at the Texas Association of Creative Writing Teacher's Conference at the University of Houston.

TEXIAN

TEXIAN was composed in response to a request from the City of Conroe & Lone Star Monument & Texas Historical Flag Park Committee, to be read at the opening, unveiling ceremonies on the 175th anniversary of the Battle of San Jacinto, April 21, 2011.

1. References to Col. Juan Nepomuceno Almonte were found in *The Texian Iliad* (University of Texas Press) by Stephen L. Hardin.

2. References to Sam Houston's encounter with the eagle on The *Red Rover* were found in *Sam Houston* (University of Oklahoma Press), James L. Haley's biography.

3. Craig Campobella is the sculptor of the statue of the Texian centered in the The Lone Star Monument and Historical Flag Park in Conroe, Texas.

HILLS
I am appreciative to Bill Sloan and his fine book *The Darkest Summer*, detailing the battles by the United States Marines that saved South Korea.

MARRIAGE LOST
For Dr. Terry Parsons Smith. The first line is taken from the Ted Hughes poem, "The Guide".

EVIDENCE
For Nancy Parsons

SIXTIES MUSIC
For Susan Portis

STEPDAUGHTER
For Laura Doehrman

FRIED GREEN TOMATOES
For my Aunt Jeanette Kierbow.

THE EDIT
For Patty Winn and others.

READING OLD HEART
For Stanley Plumly.

LAKE LADY DANCING ON THE HILL
For Shirley Schwaller 1946-2007

TWO DOGS HOWLING AT THE MOON
For my lifetime friend,Rusty Wier, a Hall of Fame
songwriter with a double-platinum song, "Don't It
Make You Want To Dance," that was included in the
sound track of the movie *Urban Cowboy*.

TRAIL MARKERS
For Jack Wilkes.

David M. Parsons, 2011 Texas State Poet Laureate, grew up in Austin, Texas and after serving in the United States Marine Corps, he attended The University of Texas and Texas State University, where he holds a BBA. After several years in business, advertising, and coaching at Bellaire High School, he received an M.A. in Creative Writing & Literature from the University of Houston. His first collection of poems, *Editing Sky*, was the winner of the 1999 Texas Review Poetry Prize and the Violet Crown Book Awards Special Citation. Parsons' second book *Color of Mourning* followed in 2007. Parsons teaches Creative Writing and Kinesiology (Racquetball and Handball) at Lone Star College and is founder and Co-Director of the Montgomery County Literary Arts Council Writers in Performance Series and Chairman of the Greater Conroe Arts Alliance. He was inducted into The Texas Institute of Letters in 2009. Parsons has four grown children and lives with his wife Nancy, an award winning Artist and Graphic Designer. www.daveparsonspoetry.com

Winner of the
1999 Texas Review Poetry Prize

Editing Sky

VIOLET ★ CROWN
BOOK
AWARDS
FINALIST

Poems by DAVID M. PARSONS

Purchase Dave Parsons' Books: http://www.tamupress.com/catalog/
CategoryInfo.aspx?cid=152

A poignant collection of intimate poems that also seem universal in
their appeal. They describe powerful experiences of an Austin child-
hood, handball, canoeing, marriage, Alzheimer's, the Marines, historic
houses, and much more. The poems draw you in and move you with
their straightforward, vivid style. When you combine the intimate im-
ages, the direct style, and the pleasing eloquence and ease of the words
and their arrangement, it makes for a truly satisfying poetry reading
experience! Like all compelling poetry, a collection you will enjoy
reading over and over.

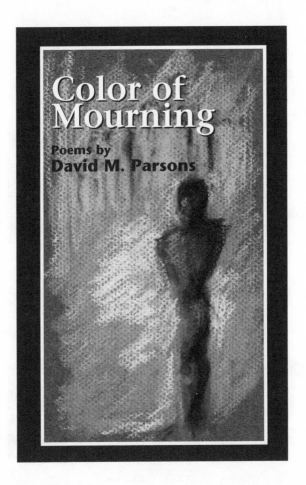

Color of
Mourning

Poems by
David M. Parsons

The reader will be taken on an odyssey including sixteenth-century England, the ancient hills of Spain, a Renoir painting in Ft. Worth, a precarious cliff side inn on California's Highway One, a rare-book library in the heart of Houston, a high-school gym in Georgia, an East Texas pine forest, and the violet crowned hills of Austin. The forays collected in this volume always return to Texas, most notably Austin, where the power of childhood memories shed light on the author's life experiences during the pivotal periods of the sixties and seventies. Examples include poems chronicling the day of the University of Texas tower sniper tragedy and the award winning poem "Night Hawk," recording the time that the poet ran face to chest into LBJ in a popular restaurant, a poem, like the writer's collection, recapturing unique and complicated times with irony, wit, and joyful mourning.

Texian

Limited Edition Prints,

TEXIAN
by David Mercier Parsons

Colonel Juan Almonte, Santa Anna's aide was the first
To call his attention to the heralding of two golden stars
Floating in their familiar field of green, white and red
Over that unlikely mission fort Alamo, small stars
That foreshadowed the larger single searing symbol
Emblazoning our ultimate flag of Texas independence
We fly so proudly today. And each of the banners
That flew over those many battles, all spoke
With the same unwavering intonation, No!
No, we will not become minions! Imagine with me
The cacophony of these many varied accents,
Of Kentucky, Tennessee, Louisiana, Alabama,
And Tejano, lilting together in the casting throng,
A composition of the most unlikely of battlefield
Symphonies, timpanis for independence.

Walt Whitman wrote in his Leaves,
*They were the glory
Of the race of rangers, matchless
With a horse, a rifle, a song, a supper,
Or a courtship, large, turbulent, brave,
Handsome, generous, proud, affectionate,
Bearded, sunburnt, dressed in the free
Costume of hunters, not a single one
Over thirty years of age.*

These were the men and boys
Of whom Walt called the *jetblack*
Sunrise at the last battle Goliad,
The same ebony tinted sun that fell on
The hardened rough hewn clay arch
Of the hallowed battlefield Alamo, where
Within the brawny breastworks of both
That simple chapel complex
And the raging men staged within
Was mirrored these same
Uniquely Texian traits.

Texian, Texian, Texian, the word
That soon returned a jetblack siesta
To the soldiers of Santa Anna
In the far flung fields of beach brush,
Mesquite, live oak, and pines
Of the San Jacinto battleground,
Texian, a word immortalized
Now the world over
By the actions of these gallant few.

Yet, these were seemingly ordinary men
With common everyday problems, desires, prejudices,
Fraught with human frailties, not ideal or perfected.
It is said that even General Sam Houston
Years before these momentous days,
Standing deeply depressed perched
Top deck on the river boat Red Rover,
Was saved from a suicidal fall by the sudden
Flash of auburn plumage as an eagle, a Cherokee
Omen foretelling a greatness to come, swooped
Auguring down toward him—

Today we stand with one of Houston's resurrected warriors
So perfectly formed by Campobella's sword, ennobled
Amongst these thirteen flags, not an hour's drive north
Of where his grand triumphant destiny brought us ours,
Where the wafting fragrances of a salty gulf coast breezes
And the pungent smoke of gun powder sweated the air
That breathed life into the fledging hopeful breast
Of a stately body to come, making legend these hallowed
Winged emblems now fully realized, as our omens,
Their bright feathers forever woven with the blood
Of these many iron willed, uniquely, soulful
Menagerie of men: these Texians.

TEXIAN was composed in response to a request from the City of Conroe, The Lone Star Monument & Historical Flag Park Committee, and was read at the unveiling ceremonies on April 21, 2011. References to Sam Houston's encounter with the eagle on The Red Rover were found in James L. Haley's biography published in 2002 by the University of Oklahoma Press. Col. Juan Nepomuceno Almonte's comments were found in the *Texian Iliad* (University of Texas Press) by Stephen L. Hardin and Craig Campobello is the sculptor of the bronze monument entitled "The Texian" that was unveiled on April 21, 2011.

Individually signed and numbered, limited-edition prints of the *Texian* poem, autographed by Dave Parsons are now available for order. These full color prints suitable for framing, display the brightly colored twelve original Battle Flags from Texas' Independence history.

Prints are available for a limited time only for **$25.00** each *(includes postage and handling)*. These keepsake 11" x 14" posters are printed on bright white card stock.

Proceeds from the sales of all prints will be used to help maintain and replace flags as needed at The Lone Star Monument and Historical Flag Park.

For more information about the park visit us at **www.texasflagpark.org**

TO O R D E R YOUR POSTER

SEND: $25.00, along with: your Name, Mailing Address, City, State, Zip Code

TO: Friends of the Flag Foundation, Inc., P.O. Box 1482, Conroe, TX 77305

CHECKS PAYABLE TO:
Conroe Live

SPECIAL INSTRUCTIONS:
Please mark on the memo line of the check: "*For Friends of the Flag Foundation, Inc*"

PRAISE for David Parsons' Poetry

I believe [a poem] to be/unlike any other/conveyance," Dave Parsons tells us in the opening lines of his new collection, *Feathering Deep*, "the manner in which/ it carries us in/ upon its own silence" to that sacred place where we can find ourselves. Think of yourself as guiding a lone canoe at midnight on some large unnamed body of water, silently feathering that vital darkness, yourself in contact with something all-embracing, sustaining and yet mysterious, a force which terrifies even as it comforts, the force which awakens you in song after song to a deeper sense of life, and you will begin to understand who this poet is who is guiding you. A big, burly Texan who speaks softly and gently, and whom you can trust to take you where you're heading and who points to those compound, familiar ghosts standing on the shore and waving."

—*Paul Mariani*, Poetry Chair, Boston College & 2009 John Ciardi Award for Lifetime Achievement in Poetry

David Parsons' *Feathering Deep* bears "the whole stamp of the human condition," as Montaigne put it: it is the work of a man who has seen a broad swathe of life, had a family, played ball, and counted fellow servicemen and musicians among his compadres. But the book is also deeply informed by English and American literature. There is no artificial barrier between art and life, love and intellect. The Renaissance man was once a courtly ideal; Parsons shows that it is a democratic ideal too—warm-blooded, muscular, as companionable on the page as in the flesh."

—*Ange Mlinko*, Winner of National Poetry Series & Randall Jarrell Award in Criticism

On *Editing Sky*—
Whether he is writing about historic houses and stately anonymous trees, or flying back—flying forward!—to reconnect to his aged father, or playing handball, or reading Kierkegaard, Dave Parsons writes with a rugged and forthright honesty, with an open-hearted freshness, with the true voice of feeling. It behooves us to listen."

—*Edward Hirsch*, Winner National Book Critic's Circle Award & President of the Guggenheim Memorial Foundation

On *Color of Morning*—
I read Dave Parsons' poetry with delight. He has high intelligence and a ready wit which make his poems unlike those of anyone who writes like him, at least in this language."

—*Robert Phillips*, Award in Literature & Creative Writing from The American Academy of Arts and Letters

US $12.95

http://daveparsonspoetry.com
Cover design: Nancy Parsons

Texas Review Press is a Member of the
Texas A&M University Press Consortium

FEATHERING DEEP
ISBN-13: 978-1-933896-79-3
ISBN-10: 1-933896-79-5

51295

9 781933 896793